ECOCRAFTS

Jazzy
Jewelry

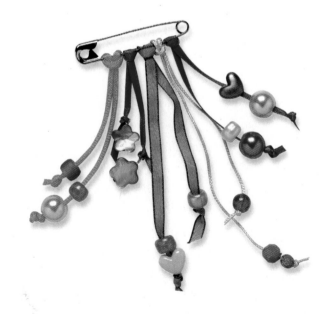

ECOCRAFTS

Jazzy
Jewelry

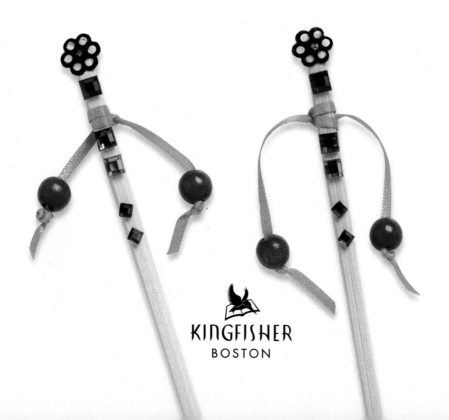

KINGFISHER
BOSTON

KINGFISHER

a Houghton Mifflin Company imprint
222 Berkeley Street
Boston, Massachusetts 02116
www.houghtonmifflinbooks.com

First published in 2007
10 9 8 7 6 5 4 3 2 1
1TR/0507/C&C/MAR(MAR)/128OJIEX-GREEN/C

Authors: Dawn Brend, Kirsty Neale,
Cheryl Owen, Melanie Williams

For Toucan
Editor: Theresa Bebbington
Designer: Leah Germann
Photography art direction: Jane Thomas
Photographer: Andy Crawford
Editorial director: Ellen Dupont

For Kingfisher
Senior editor: Catherine Brereton
Coordinating editor: Stephanie Pliakas
Art director: Mike Davis
Senior production controller: Lindsey Scott
DTP coordinator: Catherine Hibbert
DTP operator: Claire Cessford

LIBRARY OF CONGRESS CATALOGING-IN-PUBLICATION DATA
Ecocrafts. Jazzy jewelry / Dawn Brend...[et al.].—1st ed.
p. cm.
Includes index.
ISBN 978-0-7534-5969-0
1. Handicraft for girls—Juvenile literature. 2.
Recycling (Waste, etc.)—Juvenile literature. 3. Jewelry
making--Juvenile literature. I.
Brend, Dawn.
TT171.E36 2007
745.594'2—dc22

2007003560

ISBN 978-0-7534-5969-0

Printed in China

**The paper used for the cover and inside pages is
made from 100% recycled post-consumer waste.**

Contents

Ecowise

It's amazing what you can find around the house that you'll be able to turn into jewelry. By creating your own jewelry, you make sure that these items will be special to you—no one else will have jewelry that is exactly the same as the things you make.

As well as being really special, all of the projects in this book help the environment by using everyday objects found in your home. A lot of them are things that you would have thrown away. You'll find ways to turn drinking straws into a bracelet, reuse bottle caps to make a necklace, create a handbag

using wrapping paper, and even use chopsticks to make your own hair sticks. Recycling helps the planet because it reuses things that would have ended up in the trash.

Around the world, tons of garbage end up in landfills each year. In fact, in 1999 the Fresh

3 Rs to recycling

Around half of our garbage can be recycled. Follow these steps to help prevent garbage from being sent to landfills or incinerators.

REDUCE—Encourage your parents to buy products that have little or no packaging.
REUSE—Find new ways to use jars, cans, plastic containers, and other durable items.
RECYCLE—If you can't reuse something but it can be recycled, help your parents recycle it.

6

Kills landill in Staten Island, New York, became the largest human-made structure in the world, overtaking the Great Wall of China. Each year we create more garbage than the year before, and if we continue to do this, it's thought that we'll double the amount of garbage that we produce by 2020.

When we throw away so much garbage, we are also throwing away valuable resources. If we recycle our garbage, fewer materials will need to be mined, quarried, or grown, and less energy is used to transport these materials around the world. Another concern is that the landfills where garbage is buried are filling up—and there's not much space left to make new landfills.

What you can do

Save your buttons! Remove them from old clothes that are about to be given away. And look for extra buttons that come with new clothes. Buttons are great for making into jewelry.

Look for old jewelry at garage and yard sales and at thrift stores. This way you'll be helping reuse things that would otherwise go to a landfill.

Take your old jewelry to a thrift store so that it can be reused by someone else.

Save beads, jewels, and other trinkets from broken jewelry that can't be repaired. Use them to make your own new jewelry.

Pass on old jewelry that you no longer like to friends and family who might like it.

Assemble a basic craft kit, which will be useful for many of these projects. And don't forget to work in an area where you don't have to worry about making a mess.

Getting started

Before starting a project, make sure that you have everything you need. You will sometimes have to make a knot or do some sewing. If you're not sure how to do these things, follow the steps here. Some craft supplies are not supposed to be used by children under 13. If you're not sure if something is safe for you to use, ask an adult if it's okay. When using craft supplies that have a strong odor, work in a room that has plenty of fresh air. If an object is difficult to cut, ask an adult to help.

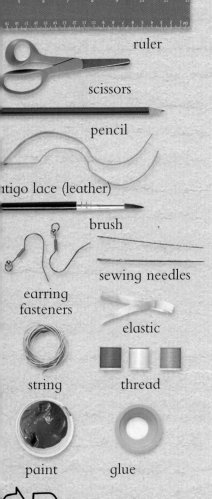

ruler

scissors

pencil

tigo lace (leather)

brush

sewing needles

earring fasteners

elastic

string

thread

paint

glue

Jewelry-Making Tips

To make it easier to thread beads onto thread or wool, dab some glue on the ends of the thread and allow them to dry. The ends will be stiff, so the beads will slide on more easily.

Make sure that the holes in your beads are large enough to take the thread, string, or elastic that you're using.

After tying a knot to finish a necklace or bracelet, dab some glue onto the knot to help stop it from unraveling.

To protect a painted finish, you can brush some glue over it and leave it to dry.

MAKING A SQUARE KNOT

You can use this knot to tie the ends of elastic together. Once you tie the knot, trim off the ends.

STEP 1

Make a simple overhand knot by bringing the ends together and feeding the left end over the right end.

STEP 2

Make another overhand knot in the opposite direction, with the right end over the left end.

BLANKET STITCH

A blanket stitch is often used to decorate the edges of fabric items, especially blankets. As well as using it for the felt change purse on pages 42–43, you can use it around the edges of felt flowers or to decorate other items such as belts and handbags. Embroidery thread works best, and you will need a sewing needle with a large eye.

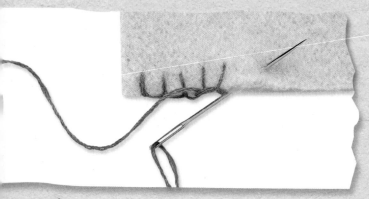

STEP 1

To start, insert the needle through the back of the fabric to the front at the very bottom edge. Bring the needle up through the back of the fabric, around half an inch away diagonally.

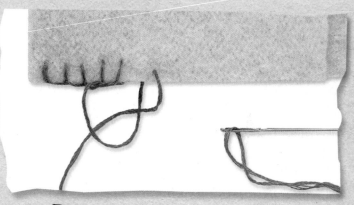

STEP 2

Bring your needle straight down, making sure that the needle goes through the loop of thread. Pull the thread until it is tight—but not so tight that the fabric bunches up.

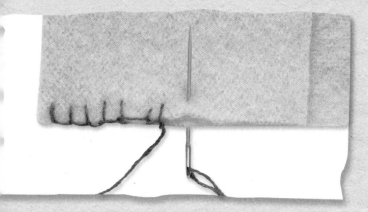

STEP 3

Take the needle to the back again and make the next stitch around half an inch away from the first stitch. Continue in this way until you finish the edge. Each new stitch will hold the loop of the previous stitch.

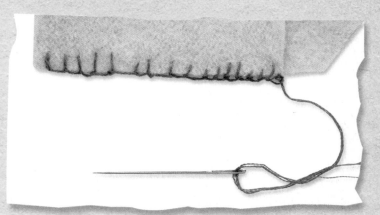

STEP 4

At the end, take your thread to the back over the last loop in order to secure it. Make a small stitch in the back of the fabric and knot it.

Cute as a button

Buttons come in all sorts of shapes, sizes, and colors, from tiny, plain buttons to colorful buttons shaped like animals. Save up lots of buttons to have plenty of choice when making a bracelet.

ECOFACT

Buttons are often made from plastic, but they can also be made from shells, silver, glass, or wood. Think about ways of reusing buttons such as for decorating handbags or T-shirts. Remove them from old clothes that you no longer wear and save the extra buttons that come with some new clothes.

YOU WILL NEED:
. . . .
elastic cord, scissors, buttons

STEP 1
Cut a piece of elastic that will fit around your wrist twice, with around 5 in. (12cm) extra. Fold the elastic in half and tie a knot in the folded end to make a small loop.

STEP 2
Thread the buttons one at a time onto the elastic, with one end of the elastic in each hole—the buttons should sit next to each other. Vary the colors of the buttons.

STEP 3
Continue threading the buttons onto the elastic until only 2 in. (5cm) are left at the end of the elastic.

STEP 4
Thread the ends of the elastic through the loop and tie a knot. Tie a pair of buttons to the ends as a finishing touch.

STEP 1

For a bracelet with fewer buttons, cut some elastic that fits around your wrist twice, with around 5 in. (12cm) extra. Fold the elastic in half and tie a knot in the folded end to make a small loop.

STEP 2

Thread both ends of the elastic through both of the holes in each button so that the buttons lie flat. Slide the buttons together.

STEP 3

Continue threading the buttons onto the elastic until only 2 in. (5cm) are left at the end of the elastic.

STEP 4

Thread the ends of the elastic through the loop at the folded end and tie a knot and bow.

Buttons that are the same size, with two holes, are the easiest to use.

These buttons are all the same size, but for the bracelet with the flat buttons, you can use one larger button as a centerpiece for it.

Friends forever

You'll only need string and beads to make this fun bracelet. Why not make two matching bracelets—one for yourself and one to give to your best friend as a friendship bracelet.

YOU WILL NEED:
....
string, scissors, ruler, glue, beads

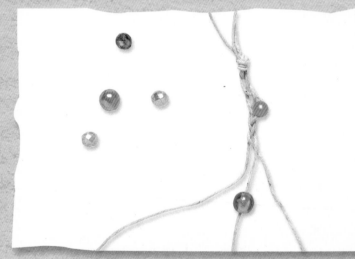

STEP 1

Cut three pieces of string 20 in. (50cm) long. Tie them together, making a knot 4 in. (10cm) from one end. To help thread on the beads, dab the ends with glue; let them dry.

STEP 2

Ask a friend to hold the knot (or hold it in the clip on a clipboard) and begin braiding—weave the strings over and under each other. Thread on a bead every inch or so

STEP 3

Continute braiding the strings until the braid is around 5 in. (16cm) long. Make a knot in the strings at the end of the braid—make sure that you pull it tight.

STEP 4

Thread a bead onto the end of a string and make a knot underneath the bead. Cut off the extra string. Repeat for all of the strings—try to keep the lengths the same.

Instead of beads, you can weave charms into the braid—or use a combination of both.

When you want to wear your bracelet, wrap it around your wrist and tie a knot at the ends.

Nice 'n' easy

Everyday plastic drinking straws can be turned into a cool anklet that's perfect for wearing at the beach. If you have pierced ears, make the matching earrings, too. Don't forget to wash the straws and let them dry before you use them.

YOU WILL NEED:
drinking straws, scissors, elastic cord, earring fasteners, thread, beads

ECOFACT
Drinking straws are made from polypropylene, which is the same type of plastic used to make yogurt containers and bottle caps. This plastic is not commonly recycled, so finding a way to reuse the straws is a great idea.

STEP 1
For the anklet, cut several different-colored straws into short lengths, around 1 in. (2cm) long.

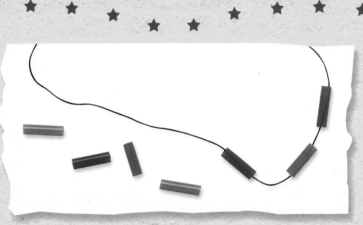

STEP 2
Cut a length of elastic that will fit around your ankle, with a few inches extra. Thread the short straw pieces onto the elastic—make sure that they don't slip off the end as you thread them on.

STEP 3
After threading on the straw pieces, tie the ends together into a square knot (see page 8) and then trim off the extra elastic.

14

STEP 1

For each earring, cut two lengths of thread, around 3–4 in. (8–10cm) long. Thread them halfway through an earring fastener and tie a knot.

STEP 2

Cut some straws into pieces that are less than one inch long. If you want the earrings to match the anklet, use straws that are the same colors.

STEP 3

Thread some of the straw pieces onto each length of thread, add a bead at the end, and tie a knot around the bead. Cut off any extra thread.

Use the same pattern of colors as shown here or choose your own color scheme.

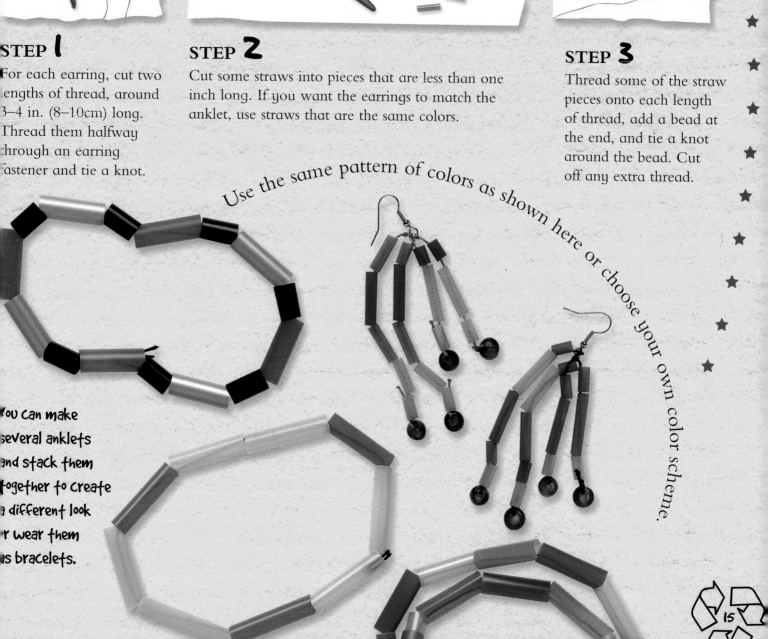

You can make several anklets and stack them together to create a different look or wear them as bracelets.

Silvery sparklers

Here's a great way to turn safety pins into jewelry. You can make a groovy bracelet and brooch that will be the envy of your friends. Use safety pins that are all the same size to make the bracelet. You'll only need one large safety pin to make the brooch.

YOU WILL NEED:

medium or large safety pins, small beads, elastic cord, one large safety pin, thin ribbon and latigo lace, charms

ECOFACT

Safety pins are made from steel and can be recycled, but reusing them will mean saving the energy needed to recycle them. If you have a new shirt, sweater, or dress, save and reuse any safety pins that are attached to it.

STEP 1

For the bracelet, thread small beads onto the spike of a safety pin almost to the tip. Close the pin. Do this for each safety pin that you're using.

STEP 2

Cut a 20-in. (50-cm)-long piece of elastic in half. Insert one length through the top fastening part of one safety pin and then through the ring at the bottom of the next safety pin, with the beads facing outward.

16

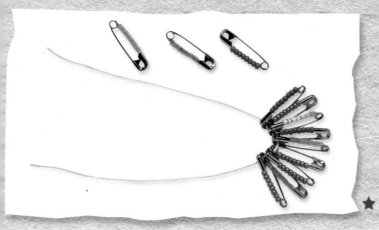

STEP 3

Continue threading the safety pins onto the elastic, following the same pattern of threading through the top part of one safety pin and then through the ring at the bottom of the next safety pin. Make sure that the beads face outward.

STEP 4

Wrap the bracelet around your wrist so that the first and last safety pins are side by side and check the fit. Add or remove safety pins if necessary. Tie the elastic ends together in a square knot (see page 8). Cut off the extra elastic.

STEP 5

Thread the other piece of elastic through the holes at the other end of the safety pins. Tie the elastic ends together in a square knot. Cut off the extra elastic.

Silvery sparklers

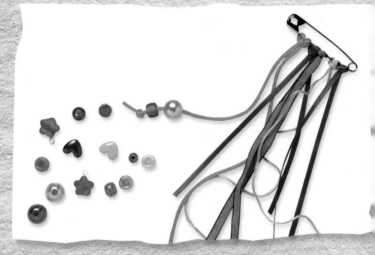

STEP 1

For the brooch, cut latigo lace and thin ribbon into lengths 4–5 in. (10–12cm) long. Fold one piece in half. Push the folded end through the safety pin. Feed the ends through the loop and pull. Repeat for all of the pieces.

STEP 2

Thread beads (make sure that they have large holes) and charms onto the ribbon and latigo lace.

STEP 3

Tie knots in the ribbon and latigo lace underneath the beads and charms so that they hang at different levels. Make sure that the knots are large enough so that the beads and charms do not slip off. Cut off the extra ribbon and latigo lace.

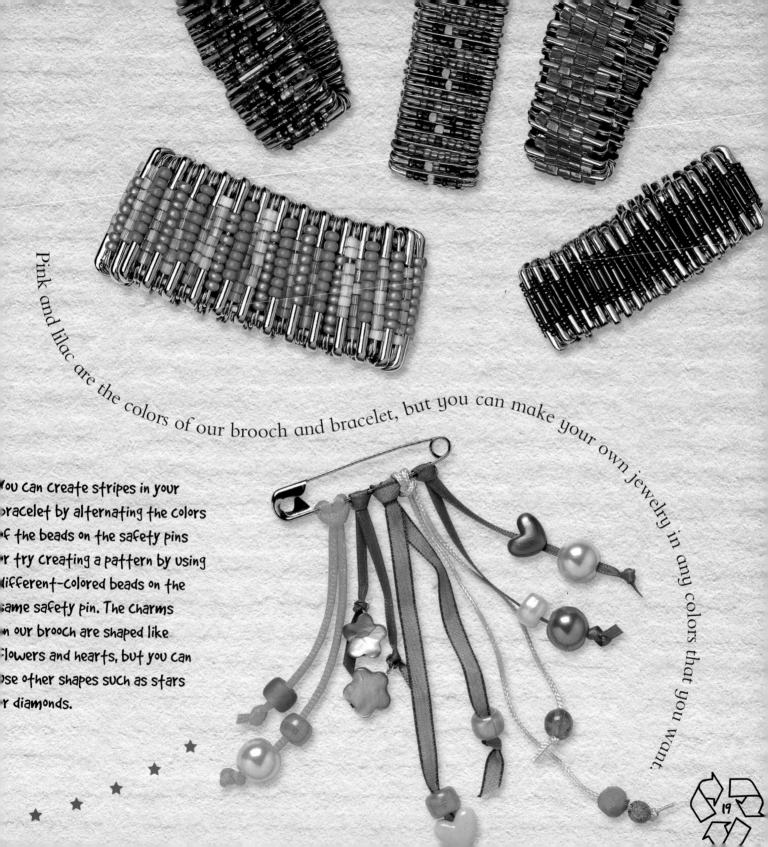

Pink and lilac are the colors of our brooch and bracelet, but you can make your own jewelry in any colors that you want.

You can create stripes in your bracelet by alternating the colors of the beads on the safety pins or try creating a pattern by using different-colored beads on the same safety pin. The charms on our brooch are shaped like flowers and hearts, but you can use other shapes such as stars or diamonds.

Flower power

Make your own corsage with leftover scraps of fabric. It will make any party dress look extra special when pinned on with a safety pin—or try sewing the back of it onto a ribbon to tie it around your wrist.

YOU WILL NEED:

paper, pencil, ruler, scissors, two contrasting fabric scraps, button, thread, needle, safety pin

STEP 1

Make two templates for different-sized flowers. Cut a 4-in. (10-cm) square and a 5-in (12-cm) square from some paper.

STEP 2

Fold a square in half along one side and then in half along the other side. Find the corner where the two folds meet. Above it, draw the shape of one petal.

STEP 3

Using a pair of scissors, cut along your outline— be careful not to cut into the folded corner. Unfold the paper, and a flower will appear. Repeat for the second template.

STEP 4

Use the large template to cut two flower shapes from a dark-colored fabric and one flower shape from a lighter-colored fabric.

STEP 5

Use the small template to cut a shape each from the dark-colored fabric and the lighter-colored fabric.

STEP 6

Place all of the flower shapes, one on top of the other, in alternating colors and with the petals staggered.

STEP 7

Thread a needle, tie a knot at the end, and feed a button onto the thread. Push the needle through the center of the petals, with the button at the top. Sew on the button tightly.

STEP 8

Gather the petals together, with the button inside, and wrap the thread around the button a few times. Tie a knot in the thread and cut off any extra.

You can use different color combinations when making your own corsage.

Attach the safety pin to the back of the corsage so that you can wear the flower on your dress. The fabric for our orange-and-yellow corsage is plain, but you can also use fabric that has a pretty pattern on it.

Chunky, funky beads

You can make your own beads by using pages from a magazine or other glossy paper. Choose the most colorful sections to create the best beads and use the beads to make original necklaces and bracelets.

YOU WILL NEED:

magazines or glossy paper, ruler, pen, scissors, glue, paintbrush, knitting needle, elastic cord or thread

Once you cut out one triangle, use it to trace around and make the others.

STEP 1

Cut out long triangle shapes from a magazine. They should be at least 6 in. (16cm) long to make chunky beads and around 1 in. (2cm) wide at the base. You can use a ruler and pen to make an outline of the shape on the paper.

STEP 2

Spread some glue on a triangle, from the tip to around three fourths of the way toward the wide base—don't glue the end.

STEP 3

Wrap the triangle around a knitting needle. Start at the base so that you don't get glue on the needle. When you reach the end of the triangle, press it down.

22

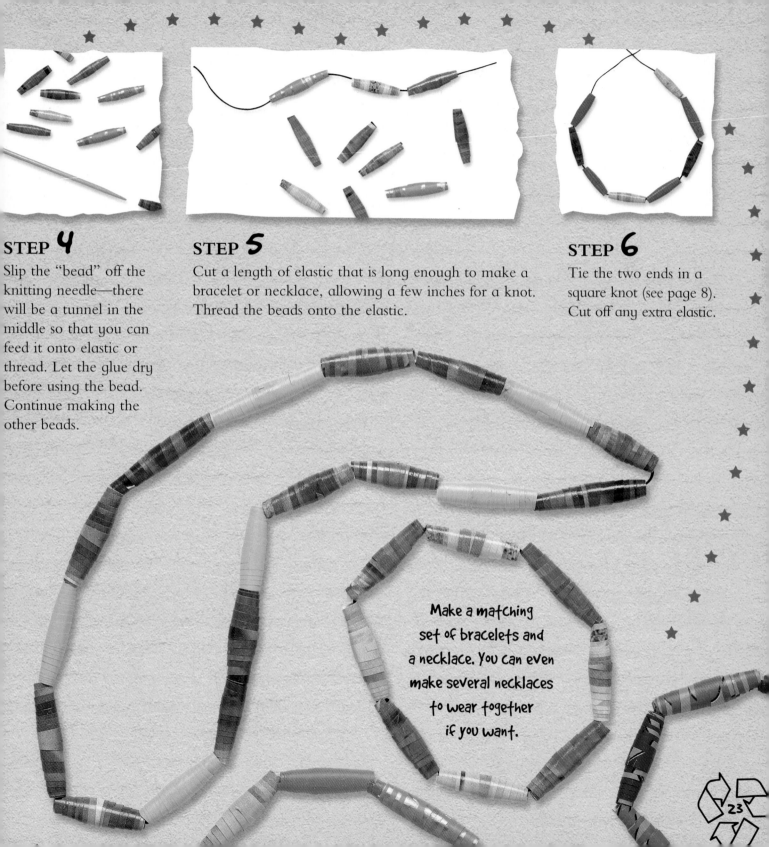

STEP 4

Slip the "bead" off the knitting needle—there will be a tunnel in the middle so that you can feed it onto elastic or thread. Let the glue dry before using the bead. Continue making the other beads.

STEP 5

Cut a length of elastic that is long enough to make a bracelet or necklace, allowing a few inches for a knot. Thread the beads onto the elastic.

STEP 6

Tie the two ends in a square knot (see page 8). Cut off any extra elastic.

Make a matching set of bracelets and a necklace. You can even make several necklaces to wear together if you want.

Picture perfect

You can turn plastic bottle caps into your own special jewelry. We're using the caps on a necklace, but you can also make them into a bracelet, brooch, or earrings.

YOU WILL NEED:
. . . .
wrapping paper, two small plastic bottle caps, one large plastic bottle cap, pencil, scissors, thin ribbon, glue, paintbrush

STEP 1

Choose sections of the wrapping paper to cut out. You can use the bottle caps as templates and trace around them with a pencil, but cut out circles that are a little smaller than the caps.

STEP 2

Cut a length of thin ribbon that is long enough to fit around your neck once it is tied. Ask a grownup to cut a pair of slits into the top of each bottle cap with a kni

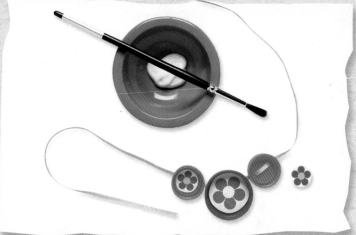

STEP 3

Carefully thread the ribbon through the slits in the bottle caps, placing the largest cap in the middle. You might need to ask an adult to push the ribbon through with a thin knitting needle or other pointed object.

STEP 4

Center the caps on the ribbon. Once you are happy with their position, glue the cut-out pictures into the caps. The pictures will also be glued to the ribbon, so you won't be able to move the caps. Let the glue dry.

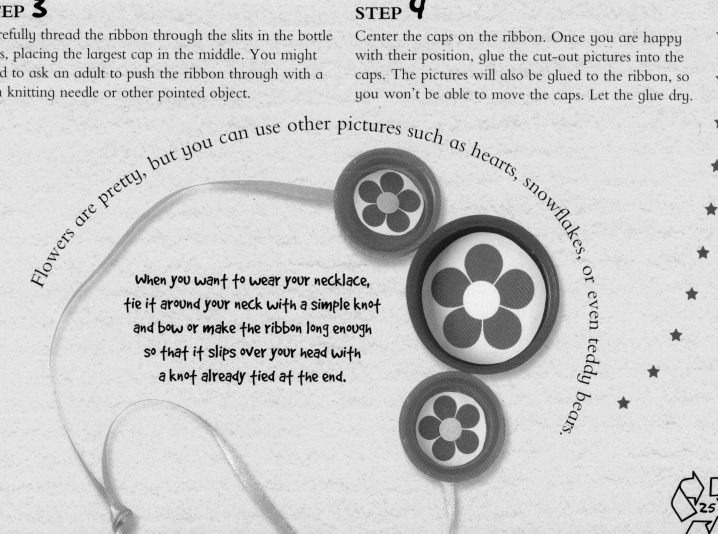

Flowers are pretty, but you can use other pictures such as hearts, snowflakes, or even teddy bears.

When you want to wear your necklace, tie it around your neck with a simple knot and bow or make the ribbon long enough so that it slips over your head with a knot already tied at the end.

25

It's a stickup!

For girls with long hair, what better way of keeping it up than by using a pair of chopstick hair sticks? The next time you have a Chinese meal, save the chopsticks. Wash them and let them dry before you make the hair sticks.

YOU WILL NEED:
....
chopsticks, fake jewels, glue, paintbrushes, thin ribbon, scissors, beads, magazines or wrapping paper, ruler, pen, gold paint

ECOFACT
Disposable chopsticks are a big reason why China's and Japan's forests are disappearing. Each year 45 billion pairs are used in China and 23 billion in Japan. In Japan, leftover wood from homebuilding is made into chopsticks, and some people carry reusable chopsticks with them.

STEP 1
For sparkling jewel hair sticks, glue some fake jewels along the wider ends of a pair of chopsticks, gluing them to all four sides and using the same colors on both sticks for a matching pair. Choose a pair of large jewels and glue one to the end of each chopstick. Allow the glue to dry.

STEP 2
Cut two pieces of thin, colorful ribbon, around 4 in. (10cm) long. Thread a bead onto each end of the ribbons and tie knots at the ends.

STEP 3
Tie a ribbon onto each chopstick, toward the end of the stick. You can wrap it around the stick two or three times.

26

STEP 1

For paper-bead hair sticks, use a ruler and pen to make outlines for two triangles, each one 16 in. (40cm) long and 1 in. (2cm) wide at the base, on a colorful piece of a magazine (or wrapping paper). Cut them out. Paint two half-inch bands of gold on the chopsticks—one at the top and one 2 in. (5cm) below the first one. Allow the paint to dry.

STEP 2

Spread glue onto the back of a triangle, completely covering it. Wrap it around the chopstick close to the top—just by the paint—starting with the base of the triangle.

STEP 3

Wrap the second triangle below the first one. Once the glue is dry, you have your beads! Cover them with glue to give them a really shiny finish.

The chopstick hair sticks are ready to wear in your hair. You can use curled ribbon to decorate a pair of hair sticks or try adding sparkling jewels to the tops of the hair sticks decorated with beads.

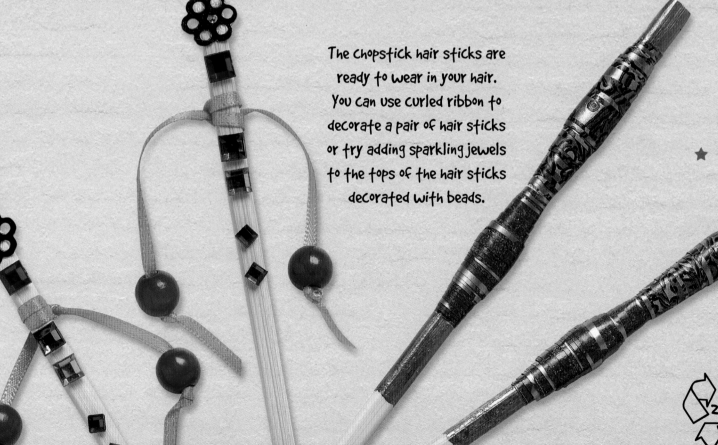

My little ponytail

Any girl with long hair will love this special hair clip. It will add color and fun when your hair is pulled back in a ponytail.

YOU WILL NEED:
cardboard tube, ruler, pencil, scissors, clean Popsicle stick, tissue paper, glue, paintbrush, striped paper, button, compass, needle, thread, tape, markers

STEP 1
Cut a 2-in. (4-cm)-wide ring from a cardboard tube. Cut through the ring and then measure 4 in. (10cm) from the first cut and cut again to make a 2-in. (4-cm) x 4-in. (10-cm) curved piece of cardboard.

STEP 2
Carefully cut out a slit at both ends of the cardboard (you might need to ask a grownup to help). These slits should be big enough to slide the Popsicle stick through.

STEP 3
Cut a piece of tissue paper that is bigger than the cardboard. Scrunch it up to make wrinkles and then smooth it out. Brush glue onto the front of the cardboard and stick the tissue paper on it. Cut off the corners of the paper. Fold in the sides and glue them to the back.

STEP 4
Add another two or three layers of tissue paper in the same way. Push the ends of the scissors through the slits in the cardboard so that they don't get covered. Brush some glue all over the cardboard and then leave it to dry thoroughly.

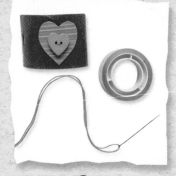

STEP 5

Draw a heart onto some striped paper and cut it out. Brush glue onto the back of the heart. Stick it in the middle of the hair clip, cover it with glue, and leave it to dry.

STEP 6

Put a button on top of the heart. Mark through the holes with a pencil. Remove the button and then make holes at the marks, using a compass.

STEP 7

Sew on the button, taking your needle and thread through the holes in the button and the cardboard. Tie a knot at the back and cover it with tape.

STEP 8

Use markers to draw stripes onto a Popsicle stick, starting with light colors. Allow it to dry and then brush glue all over to seal it. Leave it to dry.

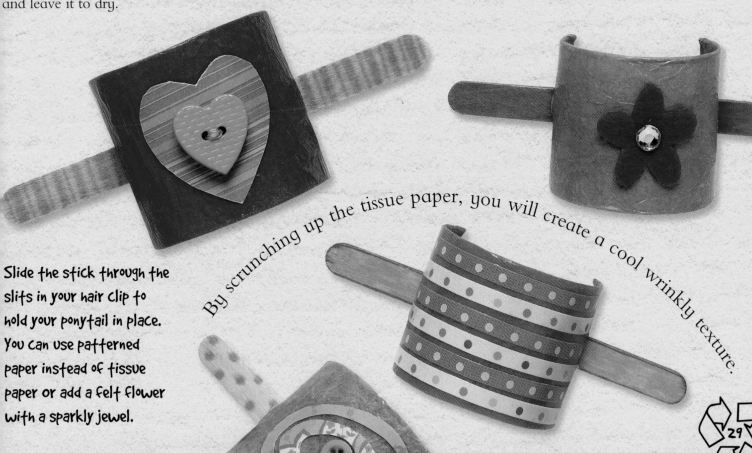

By scrunching up the tissue paper, you will create a cool wrinkly texture.

Slide the stick through the slits in your hair clip to hold your ponytail in place. You can use patterned paper instead of tissue paper or add a felt flower with a sparkly jewel.

29

Little charmers

A dangling charm hanging from your key ring will impress your friends and make it easier to find your keys. You can also use the charm to decorate your school bag or even your cell phone.

YOU WILL NEED:

wool, ruler, scissors, glue, paintbrush, buttons, key ring

ECOFACT

Metal key rings are hard to recycle, but they can be reused by taking off the old decorations and adding new ones. Some plastic key rings are made from recycled plastic, so when buying a new key ring, choose these instead of metal ones. You'll be supporting the use of recycled materials.

STEP 1

Cut a piece of wool 12 in. (30cm) long. Fold the wool in half and make a knot around 1 in. (2cm) from the folded end.

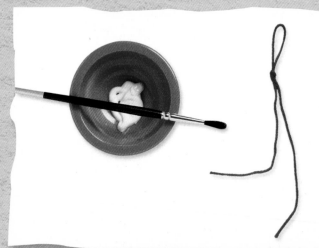

STEP 2

Dab some glue onto the cut ends of the wool to prevent it from unraveling. Make sure that the glue has dried before you move on to the next step.

30

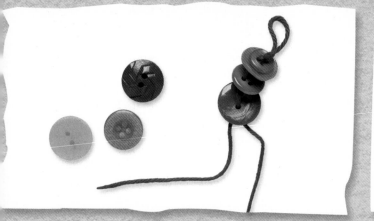

STEP 3

Feed the buttons onto the wool by threading each
end of the wool through a separate hole in the buttons.

STEP 4

Tie a square knot (see page 8) in the wool underneath
the last button. Cut off the extra wool, but leave a tassle.

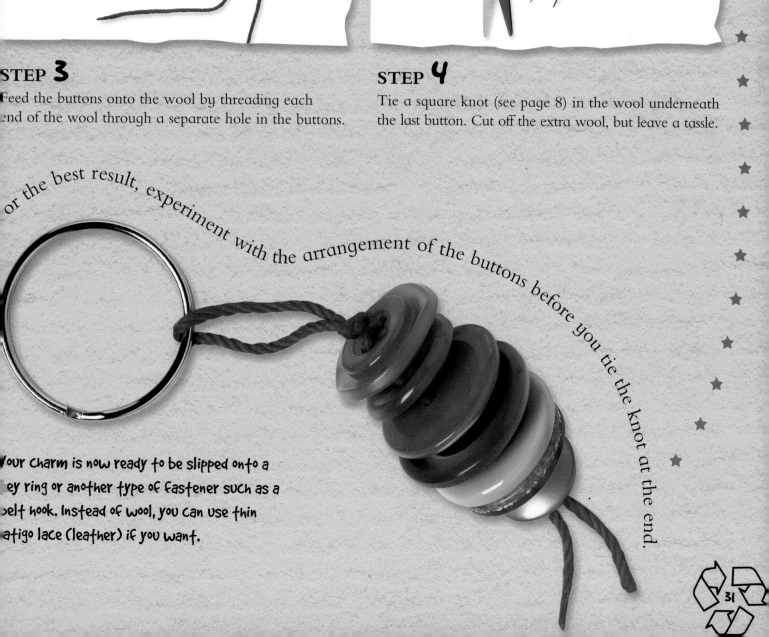

For the best result, experiment with the arrangement of the buttons before you tie the knot at the end.

Your charm is now ready to be slipped onto a
key ring or another type of fastener such as a
belt hook. Instead of wool, you can use thin
latigo lace (leather) if you want.

31

Plastic fantastic

No one will guess that this funky belt is made from plastic bags! For a longer belt, make two woven sections and join them together with a bracelet or a curtain ring.

YOU WILL NEED:

two small bracelets or curtain rings, glue, paintbrush, thread, plastic bags in four different colors, ruler, scissors, tape, paper clip, contact paper, large needle, beads

STEP 1

For each bracelet or curtain ring, dab a blob of glue onto it. Place the end of your thread down in the glue and wrap it tightly and evenly around the bracelet. Cut off the end and add a small blob of glue to hold it in place.

STEP 2

Cut seven strips of four different-colored plastic bags, 2 in. (4cm) wide and long enough to fit around your waist. You will need two strips each of the first, second, and third colors and one strip of the fourth color.

STEP 3

Tape the strips together at one end. Arrange them in this order: first color, second color, third color, fourth color, third color, second color, first color.

STEP 4

Take the left-hand strip and weave it over the strip next to it and then under the next strip and over the following one.

STEP 5

Repeat step 4, but this time start with the strip on the right-hand side. As before, weave the end strip over the strip next to it and then under the next strip and over the following one.

STEP 6

You should now have a new color on both the right- and left-hand sides. Weave these into the middle in the same way (over, under, over) as in steps 4 and 5.

Plastic fantastic

STEP 7

Keep weaving until you reach the end of the strips. Hold them in place with a paper clip. Cut the ends of the strips so that they are all even.

STEP 8

Cut a piece of contact paper 2 in. (4cm) wide and as long as your belt.

STEP 9

Fold the taped end of the woven strip around a thread-wrapped bracelet. Stick it in place by pressing an end of the contact paper, sticky side down, firmly against the woven strip.

STEP 10

Gradually peel the backing off the rest of the contact paper and press it in place along the back of the woven strip. Stop several inches short of the paper-clipped end.

STEP 11

Fold the end around a bracelet and remove the clip. Stick the plastic over the end, trimming off any extra.

STEP 12

Choose one or two of the colors and cut four more plastic bag strips 18–21 in. (45–55cm) long. Fold them in half and loop two around each of the thread-wrapped bracelets.

STEP 13

For each strip, thread it through a large needle, add some beads onto the end, and tie a knot underneath the last bead.

These belts are fun to make. You can also use thicker plastic strips and make a simple braid or make your own rings by cutting out circles from thick cardboard and painting them.

Ring-a-ding-ding

Wooden or plastic curtain rings held together with ribbon or latigo lace will make a really cool belt. We've used 11 curtain rings to create this belt, but you can adjust the size of your belt to fit you by adding more rings or using fewer of them.

YOU WILL NEED:

curtain rings, acrylic paint, paintbrush, latigo lace or thin ribbon, scissors

STEP 1

Paint dots on the curtain rings and leave them to dry. Turn them over and paint dots on the other side.

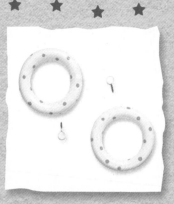

STEP 2

Once the paint is dry, unscrew the metal eyes from the rings. You might need an adult to help if they are too tight.

STEP 3

Cut ten lengths of latigo lace or thin ribbon, each one approximately 10 in. (25cm) long. You'll need around 13 ft. (4m) of latigo lace in total, including an extra piece to be used to tie the belt together.

STEP 4

Lay two rings together, side by side. Use a piece of latigo lace to tie them together with a square knot (see page 8).

STEP 5

Continue tying the rings together with the latigo lace. Make sure that the rings are lying flat, side by side, and that the knots are pulled tight.

STEP 6

Cut the extra piece of latigo lace in half. Tie each length to the end rings. Use these pieces to tie the belt around yourself.

We've shown plastic white curtain rings and blue latigo lace in the steps, but for a different look you can use wooden rings and ribbon or old shoelaces.

Wrapped and ready

Save scraps of wrapping paper to make this terrific handbag. You'll also need some denim, so this is a perfect way to reuse denim pieces that are left over if you've cut off jeans to make shorts!

YOU WILL NEED:

metallic wrapping paper, ruler, pencil, scissors, piece of denim jeans or skirt, chalk, glue, paintbrush, ribbon, large needle, Velcro

ECOFACT

The paper industry is the U.K.'s largest recycler, with two thirds of the industry taking part in recycling. You can help by buying wrapping paper made from recycled paper and use ribbon to wrap it around a present instead of tape. The paper won't be damaged and can be used again.

STEP 1

To make a folded strip, cut a 3-in (7-cm) x 6-in. (17-cm) rectangle from metallic wrapping paper. Fold it in half lengthwise and crease along the fold.

STEP 2

Unfold the paper. Then fold in both of the long edges so that they meet the crease in the center. Press firmly along the folds so that they make creases.

STEP 3

Fold the paper along the center crease again, making a narrow strip. (The long cut edges should now be hidden inside the strip.)

STEP 4

Next, fold the strip in half widthwise. Press firmly along the fold to make a crease and then unfold the last fold made in the paper.

STEP 5

Bring the short ends to the middle so that they meet the center crease. Fold the strip in half one last time.

STEP 6

This is your first finished piece, and it should be a "V" shape. Repeat steps 1–5 to make additional folded strips.

STEP 7

Each strip makes two loops. To join two folded strips together, slide one open end of one strip through each of these loops.

STEP 8

Make and add a third folded strip in the same way and keep going to create a chain with 24 strips. Make five chains.

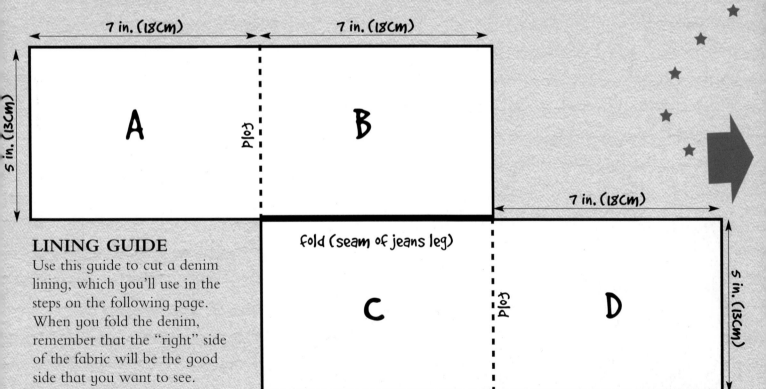

7 in. (18cm)   7 in. (18cm)

5 in. (13cm)

A   fold   B

7 in. (18cm)

fold (seam of jeans leg)

5 in. (13cm)

C   fold   D

LINING GUIDE

Use this guide to cut a denim lining, which you'll use in the steps on the following page. When you fold the denim, remember that the "right" side of the fabric will be the good side that you want to see.

Wrapped and ready

★ STEP 9

Cut out the bag lining from a scrap piece of denim. Using the guide on page 39, make an outline on the fabric with chalk. Make sure that there is a seam running through the center of the fabric.

STEP 10

Fold the lining in half along the seam. Tuck the sides inside and glue them, with the "right" side of section A against the "wrong" side of section C and the "right" side of section D against the "wrong" side of section B.

STEP 11

Glue a chain of strips onto the lining so that the points hide the bottom edge. Fold over at the sides and overlap the chain ends. Glue on the other chains to hide the denim.

STEP 12

Cut three lengths of ribbon 94 in. (240cm) long and knot them together at one end. Braid all three pieces together, weaving them under and over each other.

STEP 13

Use a large needle to
thread the braided ribbon
into one side of the bag
and then out the other
side of the bag. Tie the
ends together.

STEP 14

Cut a 3-in (7-cm) x
3.5-in. (9-cm) piece of
wrapping paper. Fold
the long edges into the
middle. Glue them down.

You can use colorful magazine pages
or candy wrappers instead of using
wrapping paper or make a smaller
chain and wear it as a cute bracelet.

STEP 15

Adjust the braided strap so
that the knot is at the top
(it will sit on your shoulder).
Wrap and glue the paper strip
around the knot to hide it.

STEP 16

Cut two small pieces of
Velcro and glue them just
inside the top edges of the
bag to make a closure.
Your bag is ready to use.

Pretty purse

An old wool sweater can be made into felt, which you can then use to make your own change purse. Ask an adult to wash the woolen item on the hottest cycle in a washing machine. Let the felted wool dry before you use it.

YOU WILL NEED:
• •
paper, pencil, ruler, scissors, old wool sweater or other woolen item, straight pins, needle, embroidery thread, buttons, string, scraps of felt

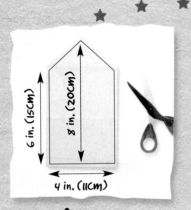

STEP 1
Cut a sheet of paper into a shape 4 in. (11cm) long at the base, 8 in. (20cm) long in the middle, and 6 in. (15cm) long at the sides.

STEP 2
Pin your paper template to the felted wool and then cut around it. Be careful to keep the edges straight. Unpin the paper and put it aside to reuse elsewhere.

STEP 3
Fold the bottom half of the rectangle up to the base of the triangle and pin it in place. Thread a needle with a length of embroidery thread.

STEP 4
Using a blanket stitch (see page 9), sew up one side and continue to the point of the triangle; leave some extra thread. Repeat on the other side.

STEP 5

Cut a piece of string long enough to make a loop that a button will fit into. Use the extra thread to sew on the loop. Fold down the flap. Use the loop to position the button and then sew it on.

STEP 6

Cut out two flower shapes, one smaller than the other, from some scrap pieces of felt. For a really cute flower, use two different colors.

STEP 7

Assemble the flower with the larger flower on the bottom and a button on top of the smaller flower. Turn the flower shapes so that the petals don't overlap.

STEP 8

Sew the flower shapes together, using the button. Now you can sew the flower onto the purse.

A contrasting color will make the blanket stitch stand out and create a funky border around the purse.

Instead of the flower, you can decorate your purse by sewing on a border of buttons or gluing on fake jewels or sequins.

43

Flowers and jewels

Open the lid of this pretty box to discover flower petals showing off your jewelry. When you do the papier-mâché, tear the pieces. The ripped edges will smooth into each other, creating a nice, neat finish.

YOU WILL NEED:

thick cardboard, ruler, pencil, scissors, packaging tape, tape, paper towels or tissue paper, wallpaper paste, pink and green paint, paintbrushes, pink felt, glue, cardboard tubes, sponge, black marker, envelopes (with patterns printed inside), thin cardboard, two buttons

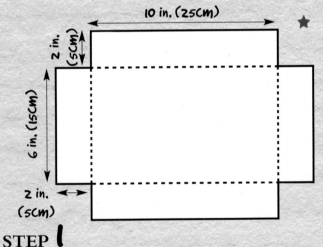

STEP 1

Use the template above as a guide to draw the box sections onto a piece of thick cardboard. Cut out the outline of the box with scissors.

STEP 2

Ask an adult to score along the dotted lines marked on the template, cutting into the lines with the blade of the scissors but without cutting through the cardboard.

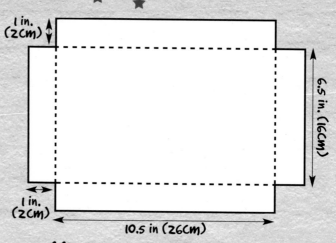

1 in. (2cm)

6.5 in. (16cm)

1 in. (2cm)

10.5 in (26cm)

STEP 3

Fold each of the four sides up and inward. Then use packaging tape to hold them together at the edges, creating your box shape.

STEP 4

Make the lid of your box, following the second template above. Draw the lid onto thick cardboard and cut out the outline of the lid. Ask an adult to score along the dotted lines.

STEP 5

Fold each of the four sides up and inward. Then use regular tape to hold the sides together at the edges, creating your lid shape.

STEP 6

Papier-mâché your box by tearing paper towels or tissue paper into pieces. Dip one piece at a time into wallpaper paste. Cover the outside of the main box, wrapping the pasted paper over the top edges. Cover the whole lid, inside and outside.

Flowers and jewels

STEP 7

When the papier-mâché is dry, paint the bottom of the box green and the top pale pink. Leave them to dry.

STEP 8

Cut some pink felt to fit inside the base of the box and around the sides. Glue each piece carefully in place inside the box. (To make your own felt, see page 42.)

STEP 9

Cut seven sections from a cardboard tube, each one around 1.5 in. (3.5cm) wide. Paint six of them pale pink and the last one bright pink.

STEP 10

Trace around the bottom of the bright pink tube onto the sponge (remove the backing if it has one) and cut out the shape. Cut three slits into the top of the sponge circle (to hold rings). Brush glue inside the cardboard tube and then place the sponge inside it.

STEP 11

Arrange the tubes inside the box in a flower shape, with the bright pink tube in the middle. Picking up one tube at a time, spread a thin line of glue around the bottom edge and press it down onto the felt.

STEP 12

Choose five envelopes with different patterns inside. Water down some of the bright pink paint so that it's runny. Brush the paint inside the envelopes (the patterns should show through). Leave them to dry.

STEP 13

Draw a large and a small petal shape onto a thin piece of cardboard and cut them out. Trace around each one five times onto the painted envelopes; cut out the shapes. Outline the petals with a black marker.

STEP 14

Glue the petals in a circle to the top of the box lid, with the smaller petals just below the bigger ones. Glue a plain button on top of each circle to make a flower center.

If you've got lots of rings, try filling more of the cardboard-tube flower petals with pieces of sponge. You could also recycle scraps of foam to make your ring holders. foam is sometimes found as part of packaging.

Index

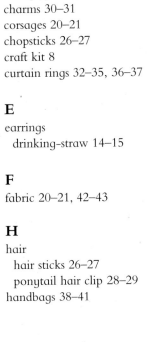